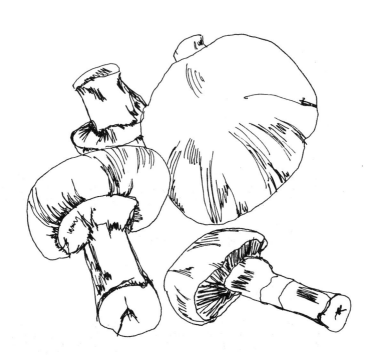

The Mushroom Growing and Cooking Book

By Alexandra Dickerman

Illustrated by Tyrell Collins

Published by
Woodbridge Press Publishing Company
Santa Barbara, California 93111

Published by

Woodbridge Press Publishing Company
Post Office Box 6189
Santa Barbara, California 93111

Library of Congress Catalog Card Number: 77–087212

International Standard Book Number: 0–912800–45–3

Published simultaneously in the United States and Canada

Printed in the United States of America

Library of Congress Cataloging in Publication Data

Dickerman, Alexandra Collins.
    The mushroom growing and cooking book.

    Includes index.
    1. Cookery (Mushrooms)   2. Mushroom culture.
I. Title.
TX804.D5   641.3'5'8   77-87212
ISBN 0-912800-45-3

Contents

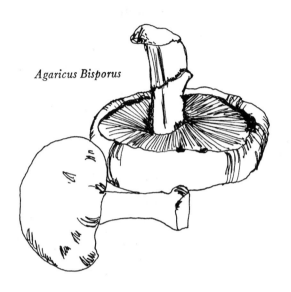

Agaricus Bisporus

Introduction

There are mushrooms of all shapes and sizes and descriptions. They range in size from almost pin-size specimens to the parasol mushroom, which sometimes has a cap measuring seven inches across and a stem twenty inches long. There are bracket fungi, which extend from tree trunks as much as two to three feet and giant puffballs measuring as large as six feet in diameter.

Mushrooms come in many colors as well: all shades of red, glorious orange, lavender or violet, and black or white. There are rare green mushrooms and some are blue. Some even change their colors. If a specimen of *Boletus Cyanescens* is broken, the white flesh changes to dark blue. Another mushroom changes to canary yellow and

7

some become black. The gills of our familiar meadow mushroom, the *Agaricus Campestris,* turn from soft pink to deep brown.

There is also a great variety of textures among mushrooms. There are mushrooms covered with slime and others with satin-soft caps. Some feel like velvet and some have hairs. There are even some mushrooms with warts.

Furthermore, mushrooms have a great variety of odors. Some smell as fragrant as flowers, some smell nut-like, and others are nauseating.

Some mushrooms even have the power to generate light, a bioluminescence.

And there is a great variety in mushroom flavors. Some, for instance, are considered among the world's greatest delicacies, and some taste terrible.

There are two familiar varieties of mushrooms available fresh from the market. On the West Coast, the *Agaricus campestris,* a white variety, is the most often seen, probably because, like white rice and white bread, white mushrooms have a popular appeal.

On the East Coast, the *Agaricus bisporus,* a very similar but brownish mushroom, is most generally cultivated. It is easier to grow, hardier and more resistant to disease. There is little difference in flavor between the two.

Then there are more exotic varieties of mushrooms, found by those who know and care, in every meadow and forest.

It is generally agreed that mushrooms are an odd and delicious plant. Their growing pattern is strange, and there is something unusual about them altogether. They even look peculiar.

If mushrooms are odd, however, they are entirely consistent with their botanical division—the fungi. Fungi do weird things, from causing athlete's foot to helping produce Roquefort cheese and alcohol. They can be pests in the house (in the form of mildew or wood rot) and yet we couldn't live without them. Even our daily bread is made through the aid of a fungus.

Yeast is one of the most wonderful and remarkable of all fungi (besides, naturally, mushrooms). It is easy to grow in small laboratories and may be one of nature's most perfect foods.

Mushrooms are usually bought and sometimes picked wild, but cultivating them at home is also a rewarding experience. Although it is not especially simple to do, growing your own mushrooms can be a delightful hobby.

But, regardless of how they are obtained, the real joy of mushrooms is in the eating.

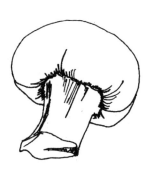

Fairy Ring

Chapter 1
The Mushroom Mystique

Mushrooms are wonderful and mysterious. Perhaps it is the way they look or the odd way they grow that is so fascinating, or it might be their delicious flavor. Whatever the reason, since the beginning of time mushrooms have been the basis of many superstititions and have captured the imagination of man wherever they have appeared.

It could very well be that the possibility of danger and the hallucinogenic properties of some of the most beautiful mushrooms historically gave them a frightening yet fascinating quality. An ancient who discovered a group of lovely mushrooms in the forest would be tempted to taste one. Would he end up with a memorable lunch, a mystical experience, or an agonizing death?

Mushrooms have been dreaded and adored, prayed to and devoured by cultures in all parts of the world from time immemorial. In Middle America, Mexico, Egypt, China, Siberia, Greece and Russia, we have evidence of ancient mushroom rituals. Mushrooms were variously assumed to possess the powers of healing, of conferring immortality, of giving supernatural strength and even of helping to find lost objects.

There are many legends about mushrooms in classical Roman literature. At that time they were considered such delicacies that a guest could judge the degree of esteem in which he was held by the quality of mushrooms his hosts served him. Later, they say Lucretia Borgia had the habit of eliminating undesirable guests by serving them poisonous mushrooms.

Some mushroom enthusiasts claim that even the biblical manna was really mushrooms, because they appear to grow in a single night and wither away at the close of the following day.

There is biblical folklore that as Christ and Peter walked through the forest eating bread the villagers had given them, wherever the crumbs fell, mushrooms magically grew.

In ancient mythology there is a frequent association of lightning with mushrooms. An old Mexican legend says mushrooms are the sacred offspring of the parents lightning and the earth. And Greek and Roman mythology both contain stories of mushrooms springing up as a result of a stroke of lightning.

Even the ancient Egyptians revered and prized mushrooms. They considered them too good for the common people and reserved them exclusively for the pharaoh. Egyptians records of more than 4,600 years ago contain legends describing the mushroom as the plant of immortality. They were most likely referring to the *Amanita Muscaria,* a beautiful red-capped mushroom with luminous white specks.

The *Amanita Muscaria* is responsible for a lot of the mysticism associated with mushrooms. This toxic, hallucinogenic mushroom has sparked religious and

Amanita Muscaria

literary imagination throughout the ages. There are even scholars who believe it was used in the ancient Greek mystery religions. It is said to have the power of mystically transporting its user, of separating his corporeal from his spiritual being and of giving him divine inspiration.

However that may be, the *Amanita Muscaria* has been included in religious lore and belief throughout the ages around the world.

Some 3,500 years ago when the Aryan people swept from the north into India, they brought with them the cult of a plant called *soma*. The juice of this plant, which was supposed to confer immortality, was drunk during religious celebrations and songs called the Vedas were written in its praise. Recent scholarship proposes that soma was actually the *Amanita Muscaria*.

In Germanic folklore the *Amanita Muscaria* was brought into the world every year when the god Wotan rode through the forest on a winter's eve, followed by his dogs and his worshippers. Wotan's retinue was chased by devils. As they all raced through the forest, the horses foamed at the mouth while bleeding from their exertion. In the following spring, beautiful but poisonous red-capped mushrooms, the *Amanita Muscaria,* appeared where the blood-flecked foam had fallen.

A carving in an ancient ruin in North Africa depicts the *Amanita Muscaria*. In ruins of the ancient city Herculaneum near Pompeii there is a painting of the *Amanita Muscaria*. An old church in France has a fresco dated around 1291 depicting the *Amanita,* which a recent scholar pointed out looks very much like a representation of the Biblical tree of good and evil.

It seems puzzling that the *Amanita Muscaria* has been so popular as a mystical symbol in so many places through the ages. Even today there are several new books on the spiritual qualities of this mushroom, asserting that it contains properties which can transport its users into the spiritual world and that the true biblical deity is in fact the *Amanita Muscaria.*

AMANITA is everywhere

The *Amanita* genus of mushrooms is responsible for much of the awe, fear and superstition surrounding mushrooms. Besides the *Muscaria*, this group includes the innocent appearing yet deadly killers *Amanita Virosa* and *Amanita Phalloides*.

The *Amanita Virosa*, or Destroying Angel, a lovely pure white specimen, is one of the most common mushrooms in any wooded area in the United States, but within 6–15 hours after the mushroom has been eaten the unsuspecting victim is suddenly seized with violent abdominal pains. The attacks come periodically until a coma develops, usually followed by death. There is no known antidote.

The *Amanita Phalloides*, or the Death Cap, is said to be the most delicious of all mushrooms. It is gray-brown in the center, fading to cream toward the edges. Victims are reported to have praised its flavor before the first symptoms appeared 12 to 48 hours later. After the characteristic painful symptoms, including abdominal pain, vomiting, and diarrhea, distorted vision and irregular pulse, the victim sinks into a coma from which he seldom recovers.

Of all the mushrooms, however, the one most responsible for the magic mushroom mythology is the *Psilocybe mexicana,* or the Magic Mushroom. It was known as the "flesh of God" to the Aztec and Mazatec Indians who used it in ancient times to produce visions and to read the future. For the Indians, eating this mushroom was, and still is, a sacred and holy event which, it is believed, can allow them to foretell the future and give advice.

The noted mycologist, R. Gordon Wasson, wrote of his experience with the mushroom, saying that after he ate several, the mushroom took possession of him and produced an effect of beautiful distortions. He writes that the walls in the room where he was lying disappeared, to be

Virosa, "Destroying Angel"

replaced by geometric patterns in brilliant colors. Then the forms took shape and became huge buildings and, he writes, his "spirit seemed to float over landscapes more beautiful than any seen on earth" and he was "conscious of a sense of deep joy."

Carlos Castaneda writes in *A Separate Reality* of his experiences with the mushroom. He tells of the Yaqui Indian belief that the drug is a guiding spirit or "ally." He reports that in order to become a "man of knowledge," a Yaqui must meet "with the ally as many times as possible in order to become familiar with it." The Yaqui explanation of the profound effects that the mushroom has on one's perceptual capacities is that the ally (or mushroom) removes a man's body.

Psilocybin, a chemical obtained from *Psilocybe mexicana,* has been used in the rehabilitation of criminals and the treatment of chronic alcoholism.

Chapter 2

Cultivating Mushrooms

If you have never tasted a freshly picked mushroom before, you are missing a big treat. And once you have mastered mushroom cultivation, which is quite different from ordinary gardening, you will be able to keep a supply of these tasty, nutritious and low-calorie treats to enhance any meal.

How to Grow Mushrooms

Mushrooms are a unique plant. They require no light to grow and in fact can withstand any amount of light except direct sunlight. They grow from tiny root-like fibers called *mycelium*. These mycelium spread throughout decaying matter. When the conditions are right, they come toward the surface and form pinheads which become, in a few days, full-sized mushrooms. If the conditions are not right, the mycelia become dormant and no mushrooms are formed. A bit of mycelium-ridden compost may be dried and stored for years, and when it is put into a moist, properly prepared compost, the mycelium will grow and produce mushrooms. The mushrooms themselves produce millions of spores which they drop in the wind. These can travel in the winds throughout the world and if they are deposited in perfect conditions they will start mycelium and eventually mushrooms. A spore from Africa can produce mushrooms in Maine. The spore process takes a long time and is chancy at best. Therefore most domestic mushrooms are grown in innoculating compost with pieces of dried mycelium from previous mushroom-growing beds or from mycelium produced in the laboratory.

Where to Grow Mushrooms

The growing tray

Garbage cans, dishpans, flower pots or boxes of practically any size may be used to grow mushrooms. However, very large trays can be hard to handle when they become filled with moist and heavy compost. Two by three feet or three by four feet wooden boxes are popular sizes. You can even use cardboard boxes, if you coat or line them with a waterproof material.

The trays should be around ten to twelve inches deep. Five three by four trays will provide 60 square feet of growing space, which will yield around 100 pounds of mushrooms in one season.

A smaller but equally successful crop may be obtained from around 24 square feet of growing space, or two three by four boxes, and they will easily fit in even a small or crowded garage or shed.

The growing box should have numerous holes in the bottom for compost ventilation.

The mushroom-growing temperature

The place where you grow your mushrooms must meet several specific temperature requirements to ensure a successful mushroom harvest.

Mushrooms grow best at around 58°F, but a room of around 52–55° will yield a slower-growing, longer-lasting crop. If the room is 62–65° the crop will be more abundant but shorter lasting.

If the temperature of the mushroom-growing room gets higher than around 72° the crop will not fruit and can easily become overrun with diseases and insects.

If the temperature falls below 50° the mycelium growth will slow down or stop completely, but it will not be killed even in freezing temperatures.

Cultivated Mushrooms

Mushrooms are grown on a bed of composted organic material. Small pieces of mycelium are planted in the compost and the mycelium start growing and spread out through the compost, filling it with stringy white fibers. At this point the compost is cased (covered with 1 inch or more of clean damp soil, peat moss or other organic material). The casing process brings on the mushroom fruiting. First pinheads (small white bumps) appear on the surface of the compost. About a week later the mushrooms start coming on in flushes. The first flush takes about four to eight days for the full-size mushrooms to form. Later flushes appear every two weeks, with each flush becoming weaker, for a total growing period of 60–90 days. At this time, the food value of the compost becomes exhausted and the mushrooms become weak and appear infrequently. Now the compost may be dumped from the growing trays and used for an excellent garden fertilizer.

Pests and Diseases

The same environment that facilitates mushroom growth also lends itself to a multitude of mushroom pests and diseases. Once these predators take hold, it is nearly impossible to get rid of them. So the wisest way to handle these intruders is to prevent their appearance in the first place.

We suggest you use a variety of strategies against these pests. First, use a good insecticide-fungicide. We use Malathion; also available from your local nursery are Zineb and Alfa-tox. However, never use these chemicals within seven days of harvest, and be sure to clean the mushrooms carefully before eating.

Between crops, completely clean and spray your mushroom-growing room. After the trays are filled and spawned, but before casing, spray the growing room—the floors, walls and all around, except the trays and the compost.

After casing, you may also wish to spray the casing surface with Malathion. Whenever any part of your mushroom crop becomes diseased, carefully remove the section which has become infected. Then sprinkle the area with lime and fill in with new casing.

The most easy and effective tool against mushroom pests is simply cleanliness. Always remove all diseased tissue and the old ends of stems after the mushrooms have been removed. Be sure there is no garbage or other breeding place in the mushroom-growing vicinity. In some cases fastidious cleanliness alone can prevent the appearance of mushroom pests and diseases.

Mushroom Compost

Compost is partially decomposed organic matter. There are many methods for producing compost and also many combinations of organic materials and chemicals which may be used to produce compost. Mushrooms require good quality compost so care must be taken in its preparation. The composting process is the result of an aerobic bacteria (one which requires oxygen to live) attacking the organic matter and decomposing it. This process takes place in nature all the time but for fast, efficient and complete composting, the temperature, moisture, air content and chemical content of the materials must be closely regulated. This allows the bacteria to breed in ideal conditions, thus causing rapid decomposition.

Sometimes you can pick up good compost from your local mushroom grower who will sell you a garbage can full and you can mix in the spawn yourself. The grower may sell you spawn or you can purchase it from mail order seed companies, or directly from laboratories which make up the spawn.

The cheapest way to obtain mushroom compost is, of course, to make it yourself. This requires careful planning, enough space to carry out the operation, and ample raw materials. The compost for mushroom growing must be of a high quality and it must be composted at a high enough temperature to assure complete composting and to kill diseases and insect larvae. Small batches of compost are the most difficult to completely compost and usually require a special insulated composter.

The major challenge for the home grower is the preparation of the compost. If you live near a horse stable or horse ranch we suggest that you use the horse manure/straw compost for your composting material. Most horse owners are glad to have someone haul away their stable refuse. But if you are in the city or an area free of horses, you will have to rely on a synthetic compost made from materials that are available in your area. The main constituent of synthetic compost can be straw or sawdust or a combination of ground-up corn cobs, newspapers, waste vegetable matter and yard clippings. Whatever base materials you choose to use, the secret to good compost is to fortify it with sewage sludge and/or urea to increase the nitrogen content so the materials can easily be composted.

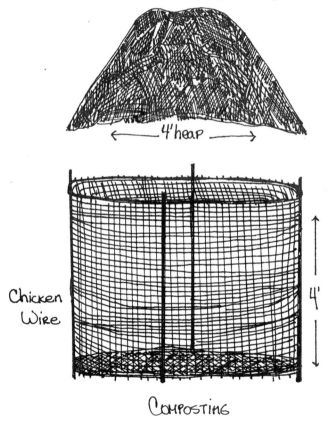

←——— 4' heap ———→

Chicken Wire

4'

COMPOSTING

Compost recipe 1

100 lbs. ground corn cobs and hay (or 100 lbs. ground newspapers and yard clippings)
20 lbs. sewage sludge
5 lbs. brewer's grains
2 lbs. gypsum
2 lbs. ammonium nitrate

Compost recipe 2

100 lbs. wheat straw
100 lbs. ground corn cobs
20 lbs. sewage sludge
10 lbs. sand
20 lbs. peat moss
40 lbs. brewer's grains
2 lbs. gypsum

Compost recipe 3—horse manure base

1000 lbs. horse manure
100 lbs. chicken manure
30 lbs. brewer's grains
15 lbs. gypsum

Compost recipe 4—chicken manure base

450 lbs. hay
450 lbs. ground corn cobs
120 lbs. chicken manure
10 lbs. ammonium nitrate
10 lbs. potash
20 lbs. gypsum

After collecting the composting materials that you have selected, mix them completely and add enough water to bring the moisture content to about 80 percent or so the water is just oozing from the bottom of the pile.

Now for the composting: the problem is to maintain the moisture content and to make sure that the entire amount of material is held for several days at a good composting temperature. There are two ways to proceed. The traditional approach is to build a compost heap about 4 feet in diameter and about 4 feet high, or to put the material in a slatted bin or chicken wire cylinder about this size. Since the outside areas of the heap will not become hot enough to compost, the entire heap must be turned inside out every three to four days. The compost will be ready in two to three weeks.

The alternative method for the serious mushroom lover who has limited space and limited time and energy for compost turning (a boring job at best) is to build an insulated composter. The trick is to build a container that is highly insulated so the heat of composting is not lost and the edges of the compost become hot enough to compost completely, and at the same time provide good air ventilation to the material so the aerobic bacteria of composting can live and multiply.

Using 2 × 4's, ½-inch-square wire screening—or mesh, and coarse sawdust and woodchips for insulation material, build a box with inside dimensions of 3 × 3 × 3 and outside dimensions of 4 × 4 × 4, thus leaving a 6-inch thick area on all sides to hold the insulating material. (See Illustration.) The top should be 3 × 3 × 6 inches thick of insulation and

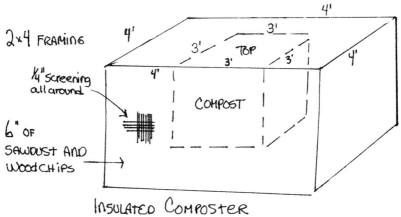

INSULATED COMPOSTER

made so that it rests on the compost and is free to move down as the compost shrinks during the composting process. There is no turning required and the composting process is shortened to seven to ten days depending on the weather and the composition of the materials.

When the compost is ready to use, the temperature will start dropping and it can be used when the temperature reaches 70–80°. The material will be dark brown, crumbly and pleasant smelling.

Filling and Spawning the Trays

Your growing trays should be set up on bricks or blocks so air can circulate below.

First press the compost tightly into the trays and smooth it down. A flat board with a handle works best for this job.

Next, you may want to pasteurize the trays by heating the room up to 130–140° for several hours. This is usually done by commercial growers but is usually too difficult for the home grower.

Your compost should smell sweet when you begin the spawning. If there is a strong odor, wait a few days until it has disappeared.

If you use brick spawn, insert small (about 1-inch) pieces 2 inches deep at 9-inch intervals.

If you are using flakes, add about one quart for every 15 square feet of compost, mixing well, before you pack the compost into the trays. Then fill the trays to the top. Wait about 24 hours, then press the compost down firmly.

If the compost starts to dry out, water it lightly with a fine spray. Be sure that water does not stand in the bottom of the trays.

After about 14–21 days, the compost will be a light gray color because it is filled with tiny white mycelium fibers.

GROWING BOX

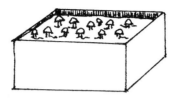

CARDBOARD BOX COATED WITH
POLYESTER PLASTIC RESIN

Casing

After the compost has been set into the growing trays and spawned, another step is required before mushrooms will appear.

A layer of material, the casing, must be placed over the compost. The casing should be around 1–1½ inches deep and can be made of a variety of substances. You can use damp, clean soil, a mixture of sand and peat moss, or peat moss and perlite, which we prefer. The casing material must remain damp, but never wet or soggy. Use a fine-misting sprayer to keep it moist.

It is important not to overwater or underwater the casing. It must never be allowed to dry out, while at the same time water must never seep down into the compost.

Harvesting

Within anywhere from five to twelve days pinheads will begin to appear. They will develop into full-sized mushrooms in about five to eight days. After that, mushrooms will reappear in flushes about every two weeks for two to three months.

Between flushes, continue to keep the beds at about 80 percent moisture, using a fine-mist sprayer whenever necessary.

Pick the mushrooms according to the way you plan to use them (see recipes which follow).

When you pick mushrooms, twist them loose, so you will pull the whole stem out. You may also wish to use a small sharp knife to cut the stem below the surface. Then fill in the holes with more casing material.

Mushroom Growing Kits

If you want to start out simply, buy a complete mushroom growing kit and just follow the directions. You can get kits from local mushroom growers or from a mail-order seed house. Kits vary in size from 6-inch flower pots to 3-foot by 3-foot wooden trays. They contain a high-quality compost with the spawn already run.

If your favorite seed company does not supply spawn and you don't have a local grower to purchase it from, you may try any of the companies listed below.

You should order dry brick or flake spawn and figure on one quart for 15 square feet of compost.

Some Spawn Suppliers

Acorn Horticulture
8018 Vicksburg Ave.
Los Angeles, CA 90045

Farron's Spawn
Kirkwood, PA 17536

Lambert Spawn Co.
P. O. Box 407
Coatesville, PA 19320

Mushroom Supply Co.
Toughkenamon, PA 19374

Stoller Research Co.
P. O. Box 1071
Santa Cruz, CA 95060

Utica Spawn Co.
2201 E. Hamlin Rd.
Utica, MI 48087

Also, check good nursery catalogs and suppliers.

Chapter 3
Basic Mushroom Preparation

Selecting Mushrooms

Choosing good mushrooms is simple. The ones with a closed cap are the freshest. As they lose moisture, the veil covering the gills pulls away from the stem to reveal the spores. Mushrooms with an open cap are more ripe and have a richer flavor than the closed ones, but the closed mushrooms are more attractive. Different mushrooms call for different effects and you should pick mushrooms to suit your recipe. Select little button mushrooms for marinating and other recipes calling for the whole mushroom. Pick large caps but not too opened for stuffing, and select the large open mushrooms for flavorful stews and sauce dishes.

Cleaning Mushrooms

There are two ways to clean mushrooms. The purists say mushrooms should be wiped with a damp paper towel, then just the tip of the stem trimmed off. The easier and more efficient method of cleaning mushrooms, which some claim will lose some of the flavor, is to hold them under a spray of cool water. Then dry them immediately. They must never be soaked as they will lose their valuable vitamins and minerals and some of their delicate flavor.

Trimming Mushrooms

The entire mushroom cap and stem is edible. Only the rough bottom of the stem should be trimmed off. When you use only the caps, save the stems for use in soups, sauces and casseroles.

Storing Mushrooms

Refrigerate fresh mushrooms wrapped in a damp paper towel or waxed paper. They keep for several days. Do not wash until you are ready to use them.

Freezing Mushrooms

Put unwashed mushrooms in a container with a tight lid. They will keep for about a month in the freezer. If you want to keep them longer, blanch or sauté them and put in an airtight container. They will keep for up to four months in the freezer if they are lightly cooked.

Drying Mushrooms

It is easy to dry mushrooms. In a dry warm climate they may be cleaned and set out in the air on newspapers. Or clean them and spread them out on trays in a slightly warmed oven until they are dried and shriveled. Store in an airtight container. They must be soaked for about 20 minutes or until moist before using.

Nutritional Value of the Mushroom

The domestic mushroom, *Agaricus campestris* or *Agaricus bisporus,* is a quite nutritious delicacy. It provides more protein than most vegetables. It is also high in B vitamins, including niacin, riboflavin, biotin, thiamine, panothenic acid, pyroxidine, folic acid, and choline. It is also a source of vitamins D, C and K.

Mushrooms are also a good source of minerals. They contain calcium, potassium, phosphorus, magnesium, manganese, copper, and chromium.

Amino acids, the building blocks of proteins, are also found in mushrooms; there are more than 12 of them, practically all man's essential amino acids, in mushrooms.

Mushrooms also contain lecithin, which helps to keep the cholesterol count down, and the enzyme trypsin, which is a valuable aid to digestion.

And one of the nicest things about mushrooms is they will not make you fat. They are low in calories, carbohydrates, and sodium. Mushrooms can be included in practically everyone's diet.

ANALYSIS OF MUSHROOM'S NUTRITIONAL VALUE

Weight grams	Measure	Vitamins B_1 mg	B_2 mg	C mg	Calcium mg	Phosphorus mg	Iron mg	Protein grams	Calories
100	¾ cup	.160	.070	2	14	98	0.7	4	36

Vitamin B complex content of mushrooms :

1 cup (3 oz.)	niacin	4.8 mg
	riboflavin (b2)	.60 mg
	panothenic acid	per 100 mg = 2.2 mg
	biotin	16 mcg.
	folic acid	100 grm = 14-29 mcg.

approximate fresh mushroom equivalents:

1 lb. fresh
{ 12 large
18-20 medium
30-40 small

1 lb. whole
{ 5 cups sliced
6 cups chopped

1 lb. sliced (cooked)   1 3/4 cups (cooked)
1 lb. chopped (cooked) . 2 cups   (cooked)

Chapter 4

Basic Mushroom Cookery

For some time we have cultivated our own mushrooms, and have compiled a selection of our favorite mushroom recipes. In some cases, as with mushroom soups, I have included several recipes. Some are simple, and others well worth the extra time and effort when you can spare it. Mushrooms may be everyday fare for quick inexpensive suppers, or may provide the most elegant haute cuisine. We enjoy them for breakfast, lunch and dinner all year long.

All the recipes that follow are meatless. The delicate flavor of the mushroom is best savored alone. Naturally, you may add meat to any of these recipes if you prefer.

The amount of herbs and spices used in any dish should be judged on the basis of your own taste and the other dishes to be served with the mushroom recipe you are

37

following. For this reason I have in most cases simply called for "a pinch" instead of an accurate measure.

Many of the following recipes call for a vegetable stock. You may use a dehydrated concentrate or canned bouillon from the market or, with very little effort, make your own delicious soup stock. Save vegetable cooking water and parings, scraps, pits and seeds. Keep them in the refrigerator until you have collected at least a pound of scraps. Then put them all in a pot with 2 quarts of vegetable water and simmer covered for about 45 minutes. Strain and store the stock in the refrigerator. You can also use various leftovers in the stock pot, including salads, grains, vegetables, bread, eggs and cheese.

Many of these recipes call for butter, especially for sautéing the mushrooms. Again, this should be varied according to the needs of your family. If you are watching calories, cholesterol and money, you may prefer to use a vegetable oil or margarine instead of butter. If you are preparing a special meal, real butter and mushrooms make an elegant pair.

I have not indicated on these recipes the number of people one dish will serve. This will depend on the size of the rest of the meal, how hungry the group is and how well they like the dish. My experience has been that you rarely have mushroom leftovers. I suggest you read the recipe through before using it, and judge according to your own experience the number of people one dish will feed.

Here are some basic mushroom cooking techniques.

How to Sauté Mushrooms

Clean and slice mushrooms. Melt enough butter to cover the bottom of the skillet. Add mushrooms, stirring frequently. Cook no more than about 5 minutes. Sprinkle with salt, pepper and lemon juice for an additional, delicate seasoning.

Grilled Mushrooms

Select large mushrooms. Clean and let them stand for one hour in warm melted butter, turning them from time to time. Season with salt and pepper. Cook over a high heat, turning once. Serve over toast with a little parsley and lemon.

Broiled Mushrooms

Clean mushrooms. Cut the stems and save for use in another dish. (If you try to pull them out do it with a twisting motion, but I always break the caps this way, so I cut the stems.) Dip each mushroom in melted butter. Broil, turning until brown on both sides (about 3–4 minutes). Sprinkle with garlic salt. Serve hot.

Baked Mushrooms

Spread cleaned mushrooms out on a cookie sheet. Pour melted butter over them and cover with bread crumbs and herbs. Bake at 375° for about 25 minutes.

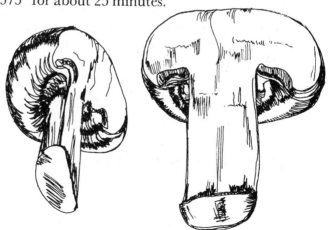

Stewed Mushrooms

Cook sliced mushrooms in a double boiler with butter, salt and pepper for about 15 minutes. Thicken the juice with flour and milk, stir and cook gently until thickened. Flavor with lemon or a little nutmeg.

Barbecued Mushrooms

Clean mushrooms. Place in center of a piece of heavy duty foil. Add butter and soy sauce. Close foil tightly. Cook on grill close to the fire for 5 minutes on each side. Serve hot.

Quick Mushroom Dishes

Try adding mushrooms, cleaned and sautéed, to:
grilled cheese sandwiches
any vegetable salad
any frozen vegetables
scrambled eggs

Try adding raw mushrooms, cleaned and sliced or whole, to:
any hot or cold soup
sandwiches of brown bread and butter, with salt and
    lemon juice
relish trays

Chapter 5

Mushroom Sauces and Gravies

Basic Mushroom Gravy

3 tablespoons butter
1 cup mushrooms, sliced
5 tablespoons flour
1¼ cups milk
Salt, pepper
1 teaspoon soy sauce

Sauté the mushrooms in half the butter for about
5 minutes. In a separate pan, heat the remaining
butter and blend with flour. Stir in the milk and
seasonings. Cook until the mixture becomes thick,
stirring constantly. Add the mushrooms.

41

Brown Mushroom Gravy

1½ tablespoons cornstarch
1 tablespoon soy sauce
1½ cups vegetable stock or bouillon
1 cup mushrooms, minced
Salt, pepper

Combine all ingredients in a sauce pan. Bring to a boil. Cover and simmer about 5 minutes over a low heat.

Basic Mushroom White Sauce

This versatile recipe makes a delicious mushroom soup if you add more milk. For any recipe calling for a white sauce, this one is probably the best. For variety, add grated Parmesan cheese.

3 tablespoons butter
½ pound mushrooms, sliced
2 tablespoons onion, chopped
1 small garlic clove, minced
2½ tablespoons flour
1¼ cups vegetable bouillon
1¼ cups milk
Salt, cayenne pepper

Melt the butter. Add mushrooms, onion and minced garlic. Cover and cook over low heat. As the vegetables begin to soften, stir in the flour. Gradually add the bouillon and milk, stirring constantly. Simmer for about 10 minutes. Season to taste.

Mushroom Puree

Use the above white sauce for a perfect puree to use as a filling—for stuffing tomatoes, eggplants, green peppers or any other vegetable, or for filling puff pastry.

1 pound mushrooms, sliced
4 tablespoons butter
Salt, pepper, nutmeg
Juice of ½ lemon
1 cup bread crumbs soaked in white sauce
½ cup Basic Mushroom White Sauce

Cook the mushrooms slowly in butter, stewing (do not fry) until soft. Add seasoning and lemon juice. Mash the mushrooms and reheat, adding the soaked breadcrumbs. Mix well and gently cook until mixture becomes quite dry. Add the white sauce.

Walnut and Mushroom Sauce

Walnuts, cream and eggs make this rich recipe especially good for entertaining. It can be used instead of white sauce, for a different effect.

1 medium onion, chopped
1 garlic clove, minced
¼ pound mushrooms, chopped
1 cup vegetable bouillon
Juice of ½ lemon
¼ pound walnuts
2 eggs
½ cup cream
Salt, pepper

Cook onion and garlic until soft. Add mushrooms. Simmer until nearly cooked. Add bouillon, lemon juice and walnuts. Beat eggs and cream together in a separate bowl. Add some of the hot mushroom mixture and then add slowly, stirring continuously, to the mushrooms in the pan. Cook gently until thick but do not boil. Season to taste.

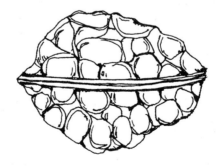

Huntsman's Sauce

This recipe uses tomato. For a hearty dish use ripe mushrooms and serve over spaghetti or brown rice.

½ pound mushrooms, quartered
4 shallots (or green onions), finely chopped
4 tablespoons butter
1 tablespoon flour
½ cup tomato sauce
1 cup vegetable stock, or bouillon
Salt, pepper, parsley, tarragon to taste

Brown the mushrooms and onions in half the butter. Stir in the flour, then add tomato sauce and bouillon. Simmer 15–20 minutes (until reduced by about a half). Remove from heat, add seasoning to taste and the remaining butter.

Duxelles Sauce

This is a classic French preserve which is used to give sauces, stuffings and various dishes a mushroom flavor. It is made with the stalks and discarded peelings of fresh mushrooms, and it is a good use for mushrooms which have become too ripe. Keep in the refrigerator in a glass jar.

3 tablespoons butter
1 small onion, minced
½ pound mushrooms, finely chopped (peelings, stalks, etc.)
Salt, pepper, nutmeg to taste

Slowly cook the onion in butter, and as it turns soft add the mushrooms. Simmer until nearly dry but not brown. Season. Cool and store in a covered jar. Refrigerate or freeze.

Mushroom Ketchup

This makes a terrific condiment and is a lovely gift, but it does require time and some effort.

3 pounds mushrooms, chopped
6 tablespoons salt
¾ cup wine vinegar
2 tablespoons onion, chopped
Pepper, thyme, bay leaf, marjoram to taste

Spread out the mushrooms in a large bowl and sprinkle with salt. Cover and leave for 2 days (stir and squash them once in a while). Put together with the other ingredients in a large pan and gently simmer for about 2 hours, until it becomes a strong concentrate. Pour through a cheesecloth into hot sterilized bottles. Cover at once and seal.

Mushroom Tomato Sauté

1 pound mushrooms
3 tablespoons olive oil
1 clove garlic
Salt, pepper, minced parsley
1 tablespoon butter
1 pint cherry tomatoes

Slice the mushrooms and brown with the garlic in olive oil. Remove the garlic and add the salt, pepper and parsley. Cook over high heat until the liquid evaporates. Add butter and cherry tomatoes. Heat briefly until tomato skins start to pop.

Mushroom Chutney

This is another mushroom condiment which is well worth
the effort.

2 cups fresh mushroom caps
2 cups cooking apples, peeled, pared and chopped
½ cup onion, finely diced
1 cup seedless raisins
½ cup crystallized ginger, finely diced
1 cup brown sugar
⅛ teaspoon cloves
⅛ teaspoon nutmeg
⅛ teaspoon cinnamon
¼ cup white wine vinegar

Cover mushrooms with water, add a pinch of salt
and boil for about 5 minutes. Add remaining
ingredients. Cover and bring to a boil. Simmer 30
minutes. Remove the cover and continue cooking
until liquid is nearly gone, about 15 minutes. Pack
in jars, cool and cover. Refrigerate. (This makes
about 2 pints.)

Chapter 6

Mushroom Appetizers

Mushroom Meringues

This recipe is different and delicious, perfect for a special occasion.

1 cup chopped mushrooms, sautéed in butter
Salt, garlic powder, pepper to taste
2 egg yolks, slightly beaten
2 tablespoons cream
Crackers
Grated Parmesan cheese
Whites of 2 eggs, beaten until stiff

Add seasonings to sautéed mushrooms. Combine the egg yolks and cream with the hot mushrooms in the pan in which the mushrooms were cooked. Continue cooking over low heat until thick—about 5 minutes. Spread on crackers and sprinkle with Parmesan cheese. Spread beaten egg whites on mushroom mixture and bake at 400° for 10–15 minutes on a lightly greased cookie sheet. If you do this ahead of time, be sure to beat the egg whites and spread them on the crackers just before baking. Serve hot.

Mushroom Surprises

½ pound mushrooms
Butter
Salt, other seasonings to taste
Pastry dough (as much as you would use for
    an 8 or 9-inch pie shell).

Sauté clean whole button mushrooms in butter.
Season to taste. Wrap each one carefully in pastry
dough, rolling into a ball. Bake on a lightly
greased cookie sheet 20 minutes at 425°.

Mushroom Turnovers

3 3-ounce packages of cream cheese, at room
    temperature
½ cup butter, at room temperature
1½ cups flour
Basic Creamed Mushrooms (see p. 99)

Mix the cream cheese and butter thoroughly. Add
the flour and work with the fingers or pastry
blender until smooth. Chill well for at least 30
minutes. Preheat oven to 450°. Roll the dough to
⅛-inch thickness on a lightly floured surface
and cut into rounds with a 3-inch biscuit cutter.
Place a teaspoon of creamed mushrooms on each
round and fold the dough over the filling. Press
the edges together with a fork. Prick the top crust.
Place on an ungreased cookie sheet and bake at
450° for about 15 minutes.

Ginger Baked Mushrooms

Add a pinch of ginger to a softened half cube of butter (not melted). Rub this mixture over fresh mushroom caps, inside and out. Place mushrooms, cap down, in a baking dish. Bake 8–10 minutes at 400°, serve hot.

Cream Cheese Caps

Mix cream cheese with seasoned salt, minced onion, parsley, lemon and pepper to taste. Fill raw mushroom caps. Chill. Serve with a sprinkle of paprika.

Tyrell's Party Dip

1 small onion, chopped
4 tablespoons butter
1 cup peeled, sliced tomato
1 pound mushrooms, sliced
2 eggs, beaten
Salt, cayenne

Brown the onion in some butter. Stir in the tomatoes and mushrooms. When cooked, mix in blender until smooth. Then return to pan, and stir in the eggs over low heat until mixture thickens but does not boil. Add seasonings. Serve as a dip or paste over crackers or toast.

Raw Mushroom Dip

½ pound fresh mushrooms, halved
2 tablespoons butter
1 tablespoon fresh lemon juice
1 green onion, minced
Salt

Place all ingredients in a blender and mix until the consistency of thick cream. Pour into a bowl and chill. Stir before using. Serve as a dip for crackers and fresh raw vegetables. To use as a sauce, warm over very low heat.

Mary Bain Sour Cream

Mushrooms may be served raw, either with salt as a low-calorie snack, or with a dip. Aunt Mary uses this dip.

Combine in a blender equal parts of cottage cheese and buttermilk. Add 2 tablespoons lemon juice.

Mushroom Butter

Sauté mushrooms and onions in butter. Mix with one cube of soft butter. Season with freshly ground pepper.

Mushroom Paprika

Sauté onions and mushrooms in butter. Add flour to thicken. Cook over a low heat, stirring constantly. Then mix in sour cream and season with paprika.

Mushroom Mayonnaise

Add 1/4 cup chopped mushrooms, 1 teaspoon mustard, and 1 teaspoon capers to a cup of mayonnaise.

Chapter 7

Mushroom Soups

Clear Mushroom Soup and Mushroom Stock

This makes a nice base for sauces and vegetable stews as well as an excellent soup.

4–6 tablespoons olive oil
1 medium onion, sliced
$2\frac{1}{2}$ cups water
1 clove garlic, minced
8 ounces sliced mushrooms
Sage, oregano, rosemary, salt, pepper, lemon juice
    to taste

Pour olive oil into a sauce pan to cover the bottom of the pan. When hot, stir in the onion and cook slowly until it becomes rich brown—not black. Pour in water. Add garlic, mushrooms, herbs and salt. We also use plenty of fresh ground pepper. Simmer for about 20 minutes. Add lemon juice to taste. Strain and serve hot.

Quick Mushroom Consommé

This is simple but it makes a very nice first course for a special meal.

2 cans consommé
1 pound small mushrooms
¼ cup lemon juice
2 teaspoons green onions, minced
Salt

Chill the consommé several hours to set. Clean mushrooms. Cut in quarters. Combine lemon juice and onions. Pour over the mushrooms. Salt to taste. Refrigerate about one-half hour. Break up the consommé in iced serving bowls. Carefully fold in the mushrooms and serve at once.

Cream of Mushroom Soup

Of the various cream of mushroom soup recipes, I prefer this because you use a blender to puree the vegetables.

½ pound fresh mushrooms, chopped
3 tablespoons butter
1 medium onion, sliced
1 celery rib, chopped
1 cup milk
Salt, white pepper
½ cup cream

Sauté the mushrooms in the melted butter, stirring until the mushroom liquid has evaporated. Add onion and celery and cook until the vegetables are soft. Pour this mixture into an electric blender. Add milk, salt and pepper. Blend about 30 seconds. Remove the blender cover and while the motor is still on, add the cream. Return this mixture to the saucepan and heat for about 5 minutes, or until piping hot.

Pumpkin-Mushroom Soup

This is a rich and unusual soup.

½ pound mushrooms, sliced
½ cup chopped onions
2 tablespoons butter
2 tablespoons flour
1 tablespoon curry powder (or less according
    to taste)
3 cups bouillon or stock
1 can (1 pound) pumpkin
1 tablespoon honey
Salt, pepper, nutmeg
1 cup milk (even better with half and half)

Sauté the mushrooms and onion in butter. Add the flour and curry powder, stirring constantly. Gradually add the bouillon. Add the pumpkin, honey, salt, pepper, and nutmeg. Cook, stirring, for about 15 minutes. Add the milk and heat, without boiling. Serve hot.

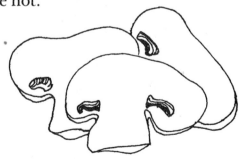

Mushroom-Lentil Soup

1½ quarts stock or water
2 cups lentils, washed
1 onion, sliced and chopped
½ pound mushrooms, sliced
Dried basil
⅓ cup oil
2 celery stalks chopped, including the tops
2 carrots, sliced
1 can stewed tomatoes
1 tablespoon vinegar
Salt, pepper

Bring the stock to a boil and slowly add the lentils.
Reduce to a simmer and cook 1 hour. Meanwhile
sauté the onion, mushrooms and basil in oil. Set
aside. Combine all ingredients, except the vinegar
and seasonings and cook at least one more hour, or
until the lentils are tender. Add vinegar before
serving. Add salt and pepper to taste.

Mushroom-Barley Soup

4 tablespoons butter
1 small onion, chopped
1 medium carrot, finely chopped
Celery, chopped, quantity as you like
8 cups stock
½ cup pearl barley
½ pound mushrooms
2 teaspoons flour
Salt, pepper, dill, parsley to taste

Melt half the butter in a large pan. Add the onion, carrot and celery. Cook gently about 10 minutes but do not brown. Pour in stock. Add barley and mushrooms. Simmer 1 hour, or until the barley is cooked. Melt the remaining butter in another pan. Stir in flour and cook to golden brown. Add a few spoons full of stock to make a smooth paste. Pour the sauce into the soup, stirring well. Simmer 20 minutes. If soup is too thick, dilute with water. Add seasonings to taste.

Chapter 8

Mushroom Salads

Basic Mushroom Salad

Button mushrooms
Olive oil
Lemon juice
Pepper, garlic, salt, parsley, chives

Slice the mushrooms thin. Mix in a bowl with oil, lemon juice, pepper, and garlic. Serve well chilled, sprinkled with salt and herbs.

Antipasto with Mushrooms

Serve a variety of raw vegetables arranged on a platter flavored with mayonnaise and lemon juice, or olive oil, vinegar and herbs.

You may choose to use:

Lettuce hearts
Celery, sliced
Radishes
Carrots, cut in sticks
Cucumbers, peeled and sliced
Peppers, cut in strips
Mushrooms, sliced
Tomatoes, cut in quarters
Avocados, cut in halves or pieces
Cauliflower (boiled 15 minutes and chilled)

Mushroom Stuffed Celery

Fill celery ribs with chopped raw mushrooms. Dress with Mushroom French Dressing.

Mushroom French Dressing

¼ cup white wine vinegar
1 teaspoon garlic salt
½ teaspoon dry mustard
Fresh ground pepper
¾ cup oil
¼ cup mushroom parts and stems, chopped

Blend vinegar and dry ingredients. Pour in oil and stir in the mushrooms. Chill in covered jar. Shake before using.

Green Bean and Mushroom Salad

Pinch oregano, thyme, salt
1 teaspoon onion, grated
1 clove garlic, crushed
¼ cup wine vinegar
1 tablespoon salad oil
1 pound small button mushrooms
1 can green beans, drained

Mix together spices, onion, garlic, vinegar and oil. Pour over mushrooms in a saucepan. Simmer 10 minutes. Add green beans and heat 5–8 minutes. Chill thoroughly. Serve cold.

Mushroom Cream Mold

1 pound mushrooms, sliced
Salt
½ small onion, sliced
1 cup water
1 envelope unflavored gelatin
1 cup sour cream
Salad greens
Cherry tomatoes

In a saucepan, combine mushrooms, salt, onion and water. Cover and simmer for 10 minutes, until the mushrooms are barely tender. Combine gelatin and ½ cup hot liquid from the mushroom mixture in a blender. Cover and blend on high speed for 30 seconds. Leaving motor on, remove the lid and slowly pour in the remaining mushroom mixture. Continue blending until smooth. Add sour cream and blend on high speed for 2–3 seconds, until well mixed. Turn into lightly oiled 1-quart mold. Chill until set. Unmold and garnish with salad greens and cherry tomatoes.

Chapter 9

Mushroom
Main Dishes

Mushroom Pizza

1 cup biscuit mix
⅓ cup milk
1 cup mushrooms, sliced
1 tablespoon butter
1 tablespoon olive oil
1 can tomato sauce
Oregano, salt, pepper
8 ounces mozzarella cheese, grated

Mix biscuit mix with milk. Roll out on floured board to form a circle or to fit your cookie sheet. Sauté mushrooms in butter. Brush dough with oil. Coat with tomato sauce, season and top with mushrooms and cheese. Bake for 15 minutes at 450°.

Mushroom Crepes

2 eggs, well beaten
1 cup milk
1 cup flour
Salt

Stir ingredients, cover and let stand at least ½ hour. The batter should be thin. Heat frying pan with salad oil and pour in enough batter to cover pan in a thin layer. Tilt pan to spread batter evenly. Cook on one side, turn with spatula and brown the other side.

As a filling, use the Basic Creamed Mushrooms recipe, p. 99; or:

¾ pound mushrooms sautéed for 5 minutes
2 egg yolks beaten with ¾ cup sour cream

Cook the ingredients together about 2 minutes. Put a spoonful on each pancake and roll up. Put in a baking dish and reheat in 350° oven.

Mushroom Chili Cunningham

½ cup onions, chopped
1 pound mushrooms and stems, sliced
1 tablespoon butter
1 8-ounce can tomato sauce
1 tablespoon chili powder
1 can pinto beans, drained

Cook onions, mushrooms in butter and add the rest of the ingredients. Serve in small bowls.

Cheese Fondue with Mushrooms

Prepare your favorite cheese fondue. Use fresh mushrooms, sautéed 3 minutes in butter, to dunk in the cheese instead of chunks of bread.

Mushroom Paprikash

1 pound medium mushrooms
¼ cup butter
1 teaspoon lemon juice
2 tablespoons onion, minced
1 teaspoon flour
Salt, paprika and a dash of cayenne
1 cup sour cream

Slice and sauté mushrooms in butter and lemon juice for 5–6 minutes. Combine onion, flour, salt, paprika and cayenne. Add to mushrooms. Stir and cook 1 minute. Add sour cream and heat but do not boil. Serve over rice or noodles.

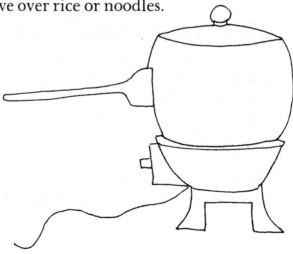

Mushroom Pie

This may be made ahead of time and reheated at 350° for 7–8 minutes before serving.

1½–2 pounds mushrooms
1 medium onion, finely chopped
Butter
Salt, pepper
½ cup Parmesan cheese, grated
1 tablespoon cornstarch combined with ½ cup
    cream
Pastry dough for 1 pie shell

Pick out the best half of the mushrooms, of uniform size, and clean them. The rest of the mushrooms should be chopped finely. Sauté the onion in butter and add all the mushrooms (whole and chopped). Season with salt, pepper, and Parmesan cheese. Add the cream-cornstarch mixture and cook slowly for about 5 minutes after

Chapter 10
Stuffed Mushrooms

Susan's Mushrooms

1 pound large mushrooms
⅓ cup butter
1 medium onion, chopped
2 cups bread crumbs
1 tablespoon catsup
Lemon juice
Salt, pepper
½ cup cream

Clean mushrooms. Remove stems by cutting carefully and chop them. Cook the mushroom stems with onion in melted butter. Stir in bread crumbs. Cook about 3–5 minutes. Add catsup, lemon juice, and seasonings. Stuff the mushroom caps with this mixture. Arrange in a glass baking pan. Pour cream around them and bake at 400° for 20 minutes.

Stuffed Almond Mushrooms

24 medium-sized mushrooms
½ cup fine bread crumbs
½ cup chopped almonds
Marjoram, salt, tarragon
¼ cup shredded cheese
3 tablespoons butter

Remove stems from caps by cutting carefully.
Chop the stems fine. Mix chopped stems with
bread crumbs, almonds and spices. Stuff mixture
into caps. Top with cheese. Dot with butter and
bake at 350° for 10 minutes.

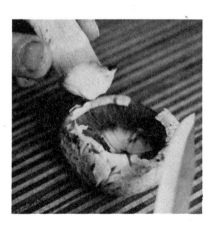

Aunt Mary Bain's Stuffed Mushrooms

Wash, dry and stem 1 pound of fresh mushrooms.
Cut off the tough part of the stems and chop the
tender parts very fine. Measure the chopped stems
and add the same volume of chopped parsley and
the same quantity of chopped shallots or little
white onions. Put it all in a piece of cheesecloth
and squeeze to extract the excess juice. Melt about
2 tablespoons of butter, add the mixture and cook
gently for 5 minutes. Sprinkle with 1 tablespoon
flour and moisten with a little broth. Cook down
until quite thick. Season to taste with salt and
freshly ground pepper, then fill the mushroom
caps and place them filled side up in a shallow
buttered baking dish. Sprinkle with soft bread
crumbs, dot with butter and bake in moderately
hot oven for about 10 minutes. Serve at once.

Rice Stuffed Mushrooms

1½ tablespoons onion, minced
1 tablespoon butter
½ cup cooked rice
¼ cup chopped nuts
Chili sauce to your taste
1½ teaspoons lemon juice
Salt, pepper
12 large mushrooms
Melted butter

Cook onion in butter until it is tender but not brown. Stir in rice, nuts, chili sauce, lemon juice, salt, and pepper. Form into 12 small balls. Remove the stems from the mushrooms and place the caps, rounded side up, in a broiler pan. Brush with melted butter and broil 2 minutes. Turn the caps over, season with salt and pepper and place rice balls in each cavity. Drizzle with butter and broil until golden.

Chapter 11

Mushrooms With Eggs

Pie Lexa

1 pound zucchini or yellow squash
½ onion, thinly sliced
4 eggs
2 cups cheese, grated
½ pound mushrooms, sautéed
Salt, pepper, oregano to taste

Steam the squash and onion until just done. Beat eggs and add to the grated cheese. Mash the squash coarsely and add to the eggs. Add the mushrooms and seasonings. Pour into a greased dish and bake covered at 325° for about 30 to 40 minutes or until set.

Mushroom Quiche

This is also good served cold, but even better reheated.

½ pound mushrooms, sliced
2 tablespoons butter
2 tablespoons onion, grated
1½ tablespoons flour
¾ cup milk (or cream)
2 eggs, beaten
Salt, pepper, freshly ground nutmeg
¾ cup cheese, grated

Sauté mushrooms in butter until tender. Sprinkle with onion, then the flour. Stir to mix. Add milk, eggs and seasoning. Stir in the cheese. Spoon into a baked 9-inch pastry shell. Bake at 350° for 45 minutes, or until golden brown and firm.

Herb Pastry Shell

Use this for your quiche if you don't already have a favorite.

⅔ cup flour
¼ teaspoon salt
½ teaspoon oregano
2 tablespoons butter

Combine flour, salt and oregano. Cut in butter until the consistency of small peas. Sprinkle about 2 tablespoons of cold water, tossing lightly with a fork. Do not overmix. Roll out on a floured surface to 11 inches round. Fit into a 9-inch pie pan. Prick the bottom and bake in 450° oven for 8 minutes or until golden brown.

Mushroom Egg Pie

6 tablespoons long grain rice
1 large onion
Sage
5 tablespoons butter
½ pound mushroom caps
Salt, pepper
3 hard-cooked eggs, peeled and cut in half
4 ounces pastry dough
1 beaten egg

Boil rice until cooked, drain. Chop onion and sage
together. Cook in butter until soft and golden.
Liberally butter bottom of a pie pan. Cover with a
layer of mushroom caps, gills up, pushed closely
together. Season. Spread rice over mushrooms,
then onions on top of the rice, then the eggs. Dab
with the remaining butter. Cover with pastry.
Brush with beaten egg. Bake at 425° for 30
minutes.

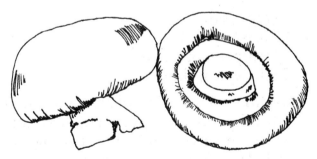

Mushroom Soufflé

1 cup fresh mushrooms, sliced
1 small onion, minced
5½ tablespoons butter
4½ tablespoons flour
1½ cups milk
Curry powder, salt pepper
4 eggs, separated
¼ cup Parmesan cheese, grated

Sauté the mushrooms and onions in 1 tablespoon butter. In a separate pan, melt 4½ tablespoons butter and stir in the flour until well blended. Heat until it bubbles, about 2 minutes. Add milk and cook until mixture thickens, stirring constantly. Add mushrooms, onions and seasoning. Remove from stove. Add beaten egg yolks. Stir in cheese. Fold in stiffly beaten egg whites. Bake at 375° in well-buttered soufflé dish for 45 minutes.

Mushrooms Stuffed with Eggs

12 large mushrooms   Milk
2 tablespoons butter   1 cup bread crumbs
4 hard-cooked eggs   Salt, pepper, grated cheese

Remove mushroom stems. Chop them and cook them in butter or oil. Shell the hard-cooked eggs. Break them into crumbs with a fork. Add enough milk to moisten (but not really wet) the crumbs. Mix up the stems with the eggs and bread crumbs. Season. Stuff the caps with this mixture. Sprinkle with cheese. Bake at 425° for 20 minutes.

Deviled Mushrooms

1 cup fresh mushrooms, minced
1 tablespoon butter
8 hard-cooked eggs
3 tablespoons mayonnaise
1 tablespoon chili sauce
Lemon juice, salt, pepper

Lightly sauté mushrooms in butter. Cool. Slice eggs lengthwise and remove the yolks. Blend crumbled yolks with mushrooms, mayonnaise, chili sauce, and lemon juice. Season well. Stuff egg halves. Chill before serving.

Mushroom Omelet

1 tablespoon butter
¼ pound mushrooms, sliced
4 eggs
¼ cup cream
Salt, pepper, nutmeg
5 tablespoons butter

Melt butter in large skillet. Sauté mushrooms until soft. Beat eggs, cream, salt, pepper, and nutmeg. Remove mushrooms from skillet and wipe it clean. Melt butter in skillet over low heat until it sizzles. Pour in eggs, cook until underside of omelet is solid. Lift sides of the omelet to allow uncooked egg to run off and cook. Put mushrooms in the center and fold in the sides to cover the mushrooms. Cook just enough to set remaining egg and serve hot.

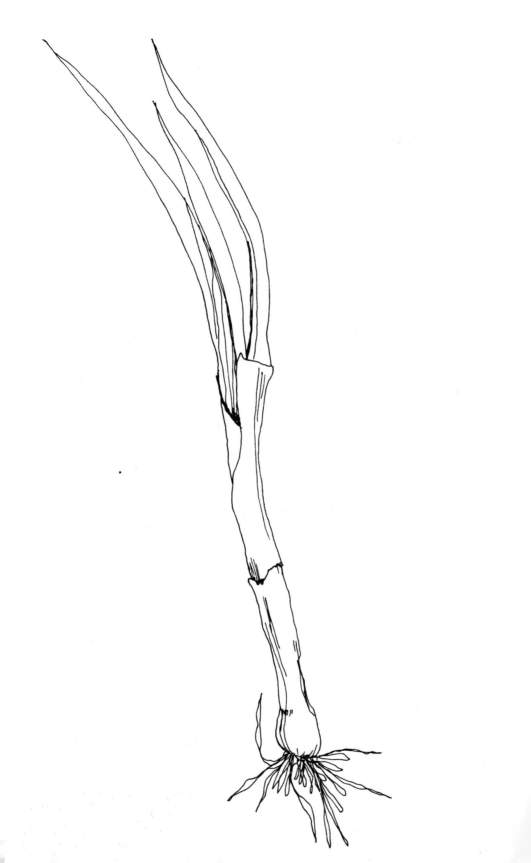

Mushroom Egg Foo Young

6 eggs
1 cup mushrooms, minced
1 cup fresh bean sprouts
1 small onion, minced
Salt, pepper
2 tablespoons butter

Beat eggs well. Stir in mushrooms, sprouts, onion and seasonings. Heat butter in skillet. Spoon in mixture to form patties. Brown on both sides. Keep hot in a low oven until ready to serve. You may like the following sauce to serve over them. This is one of our favorite quick easy meals.

Sally's Brown Sauce

Melt 1 tablespoon butter in saucepan. Combine 1 teaspoon of cornstarch with 1 teaspoon of sugar and blend into the butter. Add ½ cup water and 1½ tablespoons soy sauce. Cook, stirring constantly until mixture is thickened and bubbly.

Mushroom Eggs Cocotte

3 tablespoons butter
½ cup mushrooms, chopped
Cayenne pepper, salt
1 teaspoon flour
¼ cup broth
4 eggs

Sauté mushrooms in 1 tablespoon butter for about 2 minutes. Add salt, cayenne and flour. Cook until barely brown. Add broth, lower heat and simmer for 5 minutes. Butter four custard cups or small ramekins. Put 1 tablespoon of mushroom mixture into each cup. Break an egg in each dish, salt and place on a baking dish with a little water on it. Cook in a 400° oven for about 10 minutes or until set. Serve hot.

Mushroom Egg Creole

1 cup mushrooms, sliced
1 small onion, chopped
1 green pepper, diced
1 tablespoon oil
1 8-ounce can tomato sauce
Thyme, salt, pepper
4 eggs

Sauté the mushrooms, onion and green pepper in oil for about 5 minutes. Blend tomato sauce and seasonings with vegetables. Simmer 10 minutes with cover on pan. Add raw eggs, one at a time, to the sauce. Cover and cook until egg whites are set. Serve over hot buttered English muffins.

Green Eggs

Start with as many eggs as your family will enjoy and these other ingredients in such proportions as you prefer: cooked spinach (chopped and buttered); white sauce, butter; salt, pepper, parsley, onion juice; mushrooms, chopped and sautéed; eggs; fried croutons.

Mix the cooked, buttered seasoned spinach with white sauce. Butter custard cups or small ramekins. Put in parsley, onion juice, and some sautéed mushrooms. Add a raw egg, season with salt and pepper. Cook over a pan of water until eggs are set. Dish up hot spinach on each plate and carefully turn an egg over each mound of spinach. Top with croutons.

Baked Mushrooms

½ cup green onions, chopped
¼ cup green pepper, chopped
½ pound mushrooms, sliced
¼ cup butter
1½ cups bread crumbs
3 eggs, beaten
Salt, pepper
1¼ cups milk

Sauté the onions, green pepper and mushrooms in butter. Add the bread crumbs, eggs and seasonings. Pour it all into a greased casserole, add the milk, and bake at 350° for 60 minutes.

Mushroom Ring

2 tablespoons butter
1 chopped onion
½ pound chopped mushrooms
Salt, nutmeg, pepper, flour
½ cup milk
2 beaten eggs
Buttered green beans (optional)

Sauté onion in butter until golden. Add
mushrooms. Cook 5 minutes. Season to taste, add
flour, and then slowly add milk, stirring
constantly. Cook until thickened. Add the beaten
eggs. Pour into a buttered ring mold. Bake at
350° until firm (about 30 minutes). Turn into
serving dish and fill with buttered green beans,
if desired.

Mushroom Egg Scramble

½ pound mushrooms
5 tablespoons butter
8 eggs, beaten
Salt, pepper

Sauté the mushrooms in butter for 4–5 minutes.
Combine eggs with seasoning. Pour over
mushrooms. Cook and serve.

Spinach and Mushroom Frittata

½ pound mushrooms
2 tablespoons oil
3 tablespoons butter
½ cup minced onion
1 cup spinach, cooked and drained
2 tablespoons pimiento, sliced (optional)
6 eggs
2 tablespoons Parmesan cheese, grated
1 tablespoon parsley flakes
Salt, pepper and oregano

Slice mushrooms. Heat oil and 2 tablespoons butter in medium skillet, add the mushrooms and onion, and cook until mushrooms are slightly browned. Stir in spinach and pimiento. Set aside. Combine eggs with cheese, parsley, salt, pepper, and oregano. Beat until well blended.

Heat remaining 1 tablespoon butter in a large skillet over a high heat. Pour in egg mixture and cook until almost firm. Add spinach mixture and place under broiler to brown and set the top of the omelet.

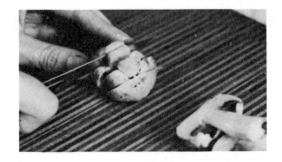

Chapter 12

Mushroom Pasta Dishes

Mushroom Spaghetti Sauce

¼ cup olive oil
1 clove garlic, minced
1 cup onion, minced
2 cups fresh mushrooms, sliced
3 cups canned tomatoes
Salt, pepper, basil, oregano
1½ cups tomato paste
2 pounds spaghetti
Parmesan cheese, grated

Heat oil in a skillet. Sauté garlic and onion until golden. Add mushrooms. Sauté for about 3 minutes. Add all the ingredients (except spaghetti and cheese) to the sauce pan. Simmer uncovered at least 40 minutes. Stir often. Serve over hot, cooked spaghetti and top with Parmesan cheese.

Mom's Greek Pilaf

¼ cup butter
1 cup canned tomatoes
1 small clove garlic, minced
1 cup mushrooms, sliced
Salt, pepper
1½ cups brown rice

Melt butter. Add tomatoes, garlic, mushrooms, and seasonings. Cook several minutes. Wash and drain the rice in cold water. Add all ingredients to 2½ cups hot water or stock, stirring only until mixed. Cover tightly and cook until boiling. Then lower flame and simmer until tender (about 45 minutes). Do not uncover while cooking and do not stir. After the mixture is cooked, let it sit, covered, for 20 minutes. Serve hot.

Mushroom Risotto

¼ pound butter
1 onion, chopped
1 clove garlic, minced
1 cup mushrooms, sliced
2 tomatoes, peeled and chopped
1 quart broth
½ pound rice
Rosemary, salt, pepper
1 cup cheese, grated

Melt 2 tablespoons of butter in sauce pan. Sauté
onion until golden. Add garlic and mushrooms
and stir. Cook 2 minutes. Add tomatoes and cook
2 minutes more. Stir in broth, rice, and seasonings.
Cover and cook gently for 25 minutes until rice is
tender. Stir. Add cheese and the rest of the butter.
Adjust seasoning and serve hot.

Mushrooms with Noodles

1 pound mushrooms
3 tablespoons butter
1 onion, chopped
½ clove garlic
1 tablespoon flour
Parsley, minced
½ cup broth
Salt, pepper, nutmeg
1 package green noodles

Separate mushroom stems and caps. Halve the caps. Chop up the stems. Heat the butter in a skillet. Sauté the onion, garlic and mushrooms about 3 minutes. Remove the garlic. Stir in the flour until you have a smooth paste. Add parsley, seasonings and broth. Gently heat and stir until thick. Mix with cooked noodles. Bake in a casserole dish about 15 minutes at 400°.

Chapter 13

Mushroom Side Dishes

Mom's Mushroom Marinade

One of the easiest and most tasty ways to serve mushrooms is whole in a marinade. This recipe makes an easy appetizer as well as a side dish to go along with the rest of the meal.

¾ cup olive oil
⅓ cup red wine vinegar
1 tablespoon chives, chopped
Tarragon, garlic, salt, cilantro to taste
1 pound small mushrooms

Combine everything but the mushrooms. Pour over the mushrooms. Allow to marinate several hours. Drain and serve.

Mushroom Marinade

½ cup olive oil
1¼ cups water
½ cup lemon juice
Salt, pepper, cilantro
Bay leaf, parsley, thyme (crushed), fennel
1 pound small closed mushrooms

Boil everything except the mushrooms for
10 minutes. Add the mushrooms and boil for
3 minutes. Chill. Serve with a little of the
marinade.

French Mushrooms

½ pound small fresh mushroom caps
Juice of ½ lemon
Salt, pepper
1 teaspoon olive oil
1 teaspoon prepared mustard
1 teaspoon parsley, chopped

Place all ingredients but the mustard and parsley
in a saucepan, cover and cook over high heat for
10 minutes, shaking often. Uncover the pan and
set aside to cool. When cold, remove the
mushrooms from the juice and blend in the
mustard. Pour the marinade over the mushrooms.
Garnish with fresh parsley. Serve cold.

Mushroom Pear Vinaigrette

1½ cups fresh mushrooms, sliced
2 pears, peeled, cored, and sliced
¼ cup vinegar
3 tablespoons water
½ cup salad oil
Pepper, parsley, salt
1 teaspoon grated onion
1 teaspoon sugar

Combine mushrooms and pears. In a separate
bowl, mix remaining ingredients. Pour over pears
and mushrooms. Cover and refrigerate several
hours. Serve chilled over crisp lettuce.

Oriental Onions with Mushrooms and Raisins

This makes a sweet relish side dish.

2½ pounds small peeled onions
2½ cups water
⅔ cup wine vinegar
1½ cups seedless raisins
1 cup sugar
⅓ cup olive oil
½ cup tomatoes, chopped (or ⅓ cup catsup)
Bay leaf, thyme, salt, pepper to taste
½ pound button mushrooms

Put everything but the mushrooms in a large saucepan. Boil uncovered about 30 minutes or until sauce is thickened. Add the mushrooms and cook 10 minutes. Serve chilled.

Mushroom Caviare

This is one of our most recent discoveries; it doesn't really taste like caviare, although the color may suggest it. But it is delicious.

1 onion, minced
2 tablespoons olive oil
½ pound mushrooms, chopped
½ teaspoon salt, pepper, lemon juice to taste
2 tablespoons sour cream

Cook onion in oil until it softens. Add mushrooms to onions. Cook for 8–12 minutes until the mixture is moist and cooked but not too soft. Season. Remove from heat. Add lemon juice and sour cream. Chill. Serve with crackers.

Sour Cream Mushrooms

½ pound fresh or canned mushrooms
2 tablespoons butter
1 cup sour cream
Salt, pepper, nutmeg

Melt the butter, add mushrooms and cover. Cook for about 8 minutes. Stir in sour cream and seasonings. Reduce heat. Cook over low heat until heated through. Makes 3–4 servings.

Mushroom Casserole

1 pound medium fresh mushrooms
1/2 cup butter
1 tablespoon marjoram
1 tablespoon chives, minced
Salt, fresh ground pepper
3/4 cup vegetable bouillon
1/2 cup cheese, grated

Put mushrooms in casserole dish. Melt butter with spices and add bouillon. Stir well and pour over the mushrooms. Sprinkle with cheese and bake, covered, for 20 minutes at 350°.

French Fried Mushrooms

12 large mushroom caps
2 eggs
2 tablespoons milk
Salt
2 cups corn flakes, finely crushed
Oil for deep frying

Clean and dry the mushrooms. Beat the eggs and milk together. Add salt to corn flakes. Heat oil. Dip mushrooms in egg and roll in corn flakes. Fry for 2 minutes to brown crust. Drain on paper towel. Serve hot. (After they are cooled they may be frozen and reheated later.)

Mushroom Fritters

Mushrooms: ¾ pound mushrooms, lemon juice, salt, pepper

Batter: 1 cup flour, 1 large egg, 2 tablespoons melted butter, ⅔ cup milk, white of 1 egg, beaten stiff

Sauce: 6 tablespoons chopped onion, 6 tablespoons olive oil, 1 can tomato paste, salt, pepper, 2 cloves garlic, minced

Cook mushrooms 5 minutes in covered pan with lemon juice and seasoning. Drain and cool. Mix batter ingredients, folding in egg white just before cooking. Brown the onion lightly in oil. Add tomato paste, seasoning, and garlic, and cook to a puree. Keep it hot. Then dip the cleaned mushrooms in batter. Deep fry (about 370°–380°) about 3 minutes. Cook in batches so you don't overcrowd the pan. Keep warm on paper towels in the oven until ready to serve. Serve with sauce.

Mushroom Croquettes

6 tablespoons butter
5 tablespoons flour
2 cups boiling milk
1 pound mushrooms, chopped
Salt, pepper
2 egg yolks
2 tablespoons cream
1 egg, beaten
Bread crumbs
Lemon juice, garlic salt to taste
Oil for deep frying

Melt half the butter. Stir in the flour and cook for
2 minutes, then add the hot milk. Cook over low
heat until a thick sauce is formed. Cook the
mushrooms in the rest of the butter and season
them. Add to the sauce. While the sauce is still
warm, beat the egg yolks and cream and add to
the sauce. Spread out in a dish in the refrigerator
to cool until firm. Form into croquettes by rolling
about a tablespoon full with the palms of your
hands. Dip in the beaten egg and then in the bread
crumbs. Deep fry for about 3 minutes until golden
brown all over. Lemon juice and garlic salt may
be used to taste. Serve hot. Or you may store them
in the refrigerator and fry at the last minute
before serving.

Mushrooms on Toast

Traditionally mushrooms have been served on buttered brown bread, usually with a white sauce, as a prized meal for the mushroom gatherer home from the forest.
Although it doesn't seem glamorous, this is one of the best ways to serve mushrooms.

1 pound mushrooms, cleaned and sliced
2 tablespoons butter
1 clove garlic, minced, or minced onion if
    you prefer
Salt, pepper, chopped parsley

Cook the mushrooms in butter, adding garlic or onion, until golden brown. Cook over fairly hot heat until most of the liquid has evaporated, but don't allow the mushrooms to stew (if there is too much liquid, just drain it off). Season with salt and pepper and sprinkle with parsley. Serve on hot buttered toast.

Quick Mushrooms on Toast

Place fried mushrooms on buttered toast. Lay slices of cheddar cheese on top. Place in oven until melted.

Mushrooms a la King

1 pound mushrooms, sliced
4 tablespoons butter
2 green onions, chopped
1 cup sour cream (or yogurt)
Salt
2 hard-cooked eggs, chopped

Sauté the mushrooms, add the onions and cook one more minute. Add the sour cream or yogurt and the chopped-up eggs. Heat but do not cook. Serve over buttered toast.

Sour Cream Mushrooms on Toast

1 pound mushrooms, sliced
3 tablespoons butter
1 clove garlic, crushed
2 teaspoons dill weed
Salt, pepper
2 tablespoons lemon juice
1 cup sour cream

Sauté the mushrooms in butter and add garlic, dill, salt and pepper and lemon juice. Cook about 20 minutes or until just tender. Pour a small amount of mushroom liquid into the sour cream, then add to the mushrooms and mix. Refrigerate about 8 hours. Heat and serve over toast or English muffins.

Sarah's Sandwich

Cook mushrooms in butter, seasoned with salt and lemon juice, for 8–10 minutes. Then put them in the blender to puree. Add butter (about 2 tablespoons for each ¼ pound of mushrooms). Grated Parmesan cheese may also be added for a delicious flavor. Serve on brown bread.

British Country Brunch

Make a sandwich of wheat bread and butter with sliced raw mushrooms flavored with salt and lemon juice.

Basic Creamed Mushrooms

There are any number of ways to use creamed mushrooms: stuffings, sauces, stews, and soups can start from one basic creamed mushroom recipe.

Cook mushrooms in butter. Add flour to thicken. Then add equal parts of broth and cream. Cook, stirring constantly until thickened (it should be like a thin paste).

Sally's Toasted Mushroom Roll-Ups

Use the above creamed mushroom recipe. Spread evenly on thin slices of white bread from which the crusts have been removed. Roll up and fasten with cocktail picks and place on a buttered cookie sheet. Bake at 375° until bread is toasted. Serve hot.

Mushroom Rolls

Cut off the top of hard, fresh rolls. Scoop out the bread inside. Fill with the creamed mushroom recipe above. Replace the tops. Place one bay leaf in each roll so it sticks out at an angle when the tops are replaced. Serve hot.

Katharine's Luncheon Mushrooms

Warm up puff pastry shells and fill with the creamed mushroom recipe above. Serve hot. They make a perfect luncheon dish.

Quick Creamed Mushrooms with Cheese

Put the creamed mushroom recipe in a baking dish. Cover with grated cheese. Bake until cheese is melted, serve hot.

Chapter 14
Mushroom Vegetable Dishes

Stuffed Acorn Squash

Cut in half lengthwise. Remove the seeds and
brush with melted butter. Place on baking sheet
with cut side down. Bake at 400° for 45 minutes to
1 hour or until tender. Then turn light side up,
brush again with melted butter, and sprinkle with
brown sugar and salt. Fill with Basic Creamed
Mushrooms (see p. 99), top with bread crumbs
and bake about 15 minutes longer.

Mushrooms with Asparagus

1 clove garlic, minced
3 tablespoons butter
½ pound fresh mushrooms, sliced
1 pound asparagus
2 teaspoons soy sauce

Sauté the garlic in butter, add the mushrooms and
sauté until golden. Cook asparagus until tender.
Combine with the mushrooms and add soy sauce.
Serve hot.

Cucumber Mushroom Aspic

2 cups water
1 bay leaf, crushed
2 teaspoons tarragon, pinch of salt
2 packages of celery flavored gelatin
    (or unflavored)
3 tablespoons vinegar
1 tablespoon onion, grated
1¼ cups cucumber, sliced and peeled (fluted)
1½ cups fresh mushrooms, sliced
Lemon juice

Boil 1 cup water, bay leaf, tarragon, and salt. Pour over gelatin and stir until dissolved. Let stand 5 minutes. Remove bay leaf. Add vinegar, onion, and 1 cup cold water. Stir. Chill until mixture begins to thicken. Add sliced fluted cucumbers and sliced mushrooms with lemon juice over them. Chill until firm. Serve on lettuce.

Stuffed Cucumbers

Wipe the cucumbers. Pare if the skin is tough. Cut into 2-inch pieces crosswise. Remove seeds and stuff with bread crumbs mixed with Basic Creamed Mushrooms (see p. 99) and grated cheese. Put in a baking dish. Surround with vegetable bouillon and bake 30 minutes at 350°.

Avocado Mushroom Bake

Fill large fresh mushroom caps with avocados mashed with freshly ground pepper, salt, lemon and garlic. Top with grated cheese and a pat of butter. Bake at 400° until cheese begins to brown. Serve hot.

Celery Oriental

Slice 6–8 large celery stalks on the bias. Cook in a small amount of boiling, salted water until just crisp. Drain. Cook 1 cup sliced fresh mushrooms in 3 tablespoons of butter until tender. Add celery and 1/4 cup sliced almond. Toss lightly until hot. Serve hot.

Cucumber Mushroom Sauté

3 tablespoons butter
2 large cucumbers, peeled and sliced
1/2 pound mushrooms, sliced
1 onion, sliced thin
1 cup broth
Salt, pepper
1/2 cup sour cream (or yogurt)

Melt butter in frying pan. Add cucumbers, mushrooms, onion. Sauté 5 minutes. Add broth, season to taste with salt and pepper. Cook 3–5 minutes longer. Take out vegetables (keeping them hot on a platter in the oven). Boil down liquid to 1/3 original volume. Remove from heat and add sour cream. Stir, pour over vegetables and serve hot.

Eggplant and Mushrooms

1 tablespoon butter
1 large onion, minced
½ pound mushrooms, sliced
1 eggplant, peeled and cubed
½ cup vegetable bouillon
½ clove garlic, minced
Salt

Put butter and onion in saucepan and cook until golden. Add mushrooms, cover and cook 5 minutes. Add eggplant, bouillon, garlic and salt. Cover and cook slowly for about 1 hour.

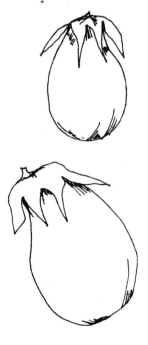

Eggplant Mushroom Soufflé

This is one of my favorites.

1 eggplant
1 slice onion
½ cup mushrooms, chopped and sautéed
1 tablespoon butter
½ cup bread crumbs
½ cup milk
Salt, pepper, nutmeg
3 egg yolks, slightly beaten
3 egg whites, beaten stiff
2 tablespoons buttered bread crumbs
2 tablespoons toasted almonds

Peel and cube the eggplant. Cover with boiling salted water. Add onion, cover and cook until soft. Remove onion. Drain and mash the eggplant. Add mushrooms, butter, bread crumbs and milk. Season to taste. Stir in the egg yolks and cool. Then fold in the egg whites. Put into an unbuttered baking dish. Sprinkle with buttered bread crumbs and almonds. Bake 30 minutes at 400°.

Stuffed Green Peppers

This is another recipe using creamed mushrooms (see page 99 for recipe). Cut off the tops of medium-sized peppers and remove the seeds and membrane. Cook in boiling water for 5 minutes. Drain. Sprinkle with salt and cool. Stuff with creamed mushrooms and grated cheese. Cover with more cheese and bake 15 minutes at 350°.

Mushrooms with Scalloped Potatoes

5 medium potatoes, sliced
Salt, pepper, garlic salt
4 tablespoons butter
1½ pound fresh mushrooms, sliced
1 cup Swiss cheese, grated
⅓ cup parsley, minced
3 green onions, minced
1 pint heavy cream
¼ cup water

Mix potatoes, salt and pepper. Blend in butter and garlic salt. In a 3-quart casserole, alternate layers of potatoes, mushrooms and cheese with parsley and onions until all ingredients except a small amount of cheese are used. Pour cream and water over it all and sprinkle with reserved cheese and butter. Bake 1 hour at 375°.

Mushroom Stuffed Potatoes

Potatoes
Basic Creamed Mushrooms (see p. 99)
2 egg yolks
Chives
Jack cheese

Clean and butter potato skins. Bake until soft at 425° for about 1 hour. Reduce temperature to 375°. Cut off the top one-fourth and scoop out center of potatoes. Mash pulp and add to creamed mushrooms. Mix in egg yolks, top with chives and cheese. Bake until cheese melts, about 15 minutes. Serve hot.

Spinach with Mushrooms

½ clove garlic, minced
½ cup mushrooms, sliced
1 tablespoon butter
2 pounds spinach, chopped
Lemon juice, salt

Sauté mushrooms and garlic in butter 2–3 minutes until mushrooms are tender. Add spinach. Cover and reduce heat when steam forms. Cook for 7–10 minutes. Add lemon juice and season.

Mushrooms and Spinach Casserole

1 pound mushrooms
3 cups fresh spinach, cooked and chopped,
     (or 2 packages frozen spinach)
Salt, garlic salt, pepper
Chopped onion
1 tablespoon butter
⅓ cup canned evaporated milk
1 cup grated cheese

Wash, slice, and sauté mushrooms. Line baking dish with seasoned spinach, onions, and butter. Spread sautéed mushrooms over spinach. In a saucepan mix milk and cheese. Simmer for 2–3 minutes. Pour slightly cooled sauce over mushrooms, and bake for 20 minutes at 350°. Then broil until top is brown.

Wilted Spinach with Mushrooms

1 pound spinach
½ pound mushrooms
¼ cup vinegar
½ teaspoon salt
2 cloves of garlic, minced
Pepper, oregano, dry mustard, basil
½ teaspoon sugar
Pat of butter
1 tablespoon TVP bacon bits

Clean spinach, tear off leaves and drain on paper towels. Slice mushrooms and combine with spinach in a bowl. In a separate bowl mix vinegar and spices. Heat the vinegar mixture in melted butter in a saucepan. Then pour it over the spinach and mushrooms. Toss well. Sprinkle with bacon bits and serve at once.

Mushroom Stuffed Tomatoes

1 cup small, whole button mushrooms
4 large firm tomatoes
Mayonnaise, as you like
1 pint cottage cheese
3 green onions or scallions, chopped
1 teaspoon celery salt
¼ cup olive oil

Simmer mushrooms for 5 minutes in lightly salted water. Drain and cool. Remove tops from tomatoes. Scoop out about half the pulp. Mix mayonnaise, cottage cheese, onions, mushrooms, celery salt and olive oil. Stuff tomatoes with mixture. Serve chilled on lettuce.

Stuffed Zucchini

1 pound zucchini
Butter
1 small onion, chopped
½ pound mushrooms
Canned peeled tomatoes, quantity as you prefer
Parmesan cheese, salt, pepper, parsley, oregano
⅓ cup bread crumbs

Wash zucchini and put it into a pan of boiling
water so it is covered with water (not salted). Cook
gently for about 10–15 minutes until tender but
not soft. Drain and cool. Cut lengthwise, remove
pulp carefully and mash it up. In a saucepan sauté
the onion and mushrooms in butter. Add zucchini
pulp, tomatoes, cheese, seasoning and bread
crumbs. Cook for about 7 minutes. Brush zucchini
with butter and salt lightly. Stuff with mushroom
mixture. Dot with butter pieces and bake for 30
minutes at 350°.

Stir-Fry Mushrooms

1 small cauliflower, broken into flowerettes
1 zucchini, sliced
6 green onions, chopped
2 carrots, sliced
4 stalks celery, sliced
1 cup mushrooms, sliced
½ cube butter
2 tablespoons water
1 tablespoon vegetable bouillon
Soy sauce
Toasted sesame seed

Combine vegetables. Melt butter in large frying
pan (or wok). Add vegetables and sauté for
5 minutes, tossing gently. Add water and bouillon.
Cover and simmer for 1–2 minutes. Toss, serve hot
with soy sauce. Sprinkle with sesame seed.

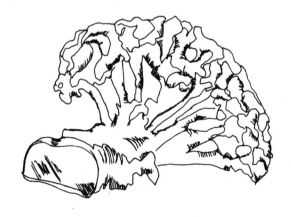

Grandma Doris' Zucchini Supreme

4 cups zucchini, sliced
1 cup mushrooms, sliced and sautéed
1 medium onion, sliced and separated into rings
½ cup green pepper, chopped
1 8-ounce package of sliced, processed American
    cheese
3 eggs, beaten
3 cups croutons, soaked in butter

Layer the zucchini, mushrooms, onions, and
peppers alternately in a 9″ × 13″ greased pan.
Cover with the cheese. Then pour in eggs and
cover with the croutons. Put on the lid and bake
45 minutes at 350°, then uncover and bake
15 minutes longer.

Mushroom Chow Mein

1 cup broth
1 cup celery, diced
1 cup carrots, diced
1 cup peas (Chinese or fresh)
1½ teaspoons soy sauce
4-ounce can of Chinese dried noodles
Rosemary, salt, pepper
3 tablespoons oil
1 cup onions, slivered
1 cup mushrooms, diced
3 tablespoons flour

Simmer celery in broth for 3–5 minutes, then add
carrots and peas. Season well. Cook covered for
10 minutes. Sauté onions in hot oil until soft. Toss in
mushrooms for a few minutes. Blend flour in a
separate dish with ¼ cup of cold water. Add to
vegetables. Add onions and mushrooms. Stir until
sauce thickens. Bring to boil. Serve hot over noodles.

A Mushroom Dessert!

Mary McHugh's Mushroom Macaroons

Mushrooms seem to keep these cookies wonderfully moist. This is a unique cookie recipe!

Butter a cookie sheet. Set oven at 300°.

1 can sweetened condensed milk
1 cup shredded coconut
1/4 teaspoon salt
1 cup mushrooms, cut small
1 cup chopped nuts
1 teaspoon vanilla

Mix ingredients. Spoon onto cookie sheet. Bake 25–30 minutes, or until golden and firm.

Shiitake

Chapter 15
Specialty Mushrooms

There are several truly delicious mushrooms available dried or in cans from specialty shops. These are well worth discovering. All of the mushroom recipes in the recipe section are suited to these varieties, which will add a different flavor to the dish according to the type of mushroom you use. In case of the more flavorful types, use fewer mushrooms than called for.

SHIITAKE
(Lentinus edodes)

Shiitake can be bought dried from Japan where they are cultivated on logs of oak and other trees like the *shii* (hence *shii* mushrooms, or shiitake). The shiitake is the most popular mushroom in Oriental cookery. The Japanese export more than 3 million pounds a year to countries all over the world, including China.

Shiitake Preparation

Shiitake are dried whole. They vary in size from one-half inch across to about two inches. Underneath the caps, the gills are a light tan mass of fine pleating. Their caps are brown on top and wrinkled or slashed apart. The shiitake are distinctive in their taste as well as appearance and they have a strong flavor and a firm chewy texture.

Shiitake require prolonged and laborious cultivation. As a result they are more expensive than our domestic mushrooms. Because of their price and the strong flavor shiitake are used by the "count" (a recipe calls for a specific number of mushrooms rather than by the pound).

Shiitake are used as a seasoning and considered a luxury—to be enjoyed sparingly. Besides their good texture, they retain their own flavor as well as enhancing the flavor of the foods with which they are cooked.

Shiitake should be soaked, cap down, for about 20 minutes, covered with cold water. When nearly all the water is absorbed, the mushrooms will be softened and pliable. Save the excess water to use, as it is rich in nutrients. The stalks should be discarded. You may want

Shiitake

to save a few caps whole after the rest are sliced, halved or quartered to use as a garnish.

In an oriental grocery store there will probably only be two kinds of dried imported mushrooms available, the shiitake and the more expensive and rarer mushrooms, the wood ears. You can tell which are shiitake by the price and the look of the mushrooms, although their names may vary. The wood ears are black and look like a mass of charred wood.

Shiitake Recipes

Shiitake can be fried, baked with stuffing, steamed, or substituted for regular cultivated mushrooms.

Here are some of our favorite recipes:

Shiitake Cucumber Sauté

1 cucumber
6 shiitake
4 tablespoons sesame seeds
4 tablespoons oil
4 teaspoons sugar
6 tablespoons soy sauce

Slice the cucumber and sprinkle it with salt and drain. Slice the mushrooms. Toast about
4 tablespoons of sesame seeds in a dry frying pan, stirring until the seeds pop. Heat oil in pan and add cucumbers and mushrooms. Cook until cucumbers begin to soften. Add sugar and soy sauce, stirring and cooking for about 1 minute.

Creamed Shiitake

We like this over toast, baked potatoes, vegetables, or rice.

Butter and salt
4–6 shiitake (soaked, drained, and sliced)
1 cup white sauce
Pinch of parsley

Melt butter in a frying pan to the point at which it gives off a fragrance. Sauté the mushrooms until they become soft. Add to white sauce. Season to taste. Garnish with parsley.

Shiitake Omelet

Soak, slice and sauté in butter 4–6 medium shiitake mushrooms. Add to a four-egg omelet and add a little cheese if desired.

Shiitake Eggplant

1 pound eggplant (peeled, diced, and salted)
Cooking oil
4–5 shiitake caps (soaked, stemmed, and
     quartered)
1 cup walnuts, chopped
½ cup almonds, chopped
⅛ cup soy sauce
2 tablespoons sugar

Fry the eggplant in oil. Add mushrooms and nuts. Mix in remaining ingredients. Cook until well heated. Serve piping hot.

MOREL, MERKEL, SPONGE MUSHROOM
(Morchella esculenta and *Morchella vulgaris)*

These mushrooms come dried or canned from France. They are usually split down the center or sliced. Wash them thoroughly to clean out dirt in the crevices. Use a handful of salt in the washing water.

Morels can be fried but they are best creamed (see Basic Creamed Mushrooms, p. 99).

CEP, CÈPE
(Boletus edulis)

To cook ceps, fry them (preferably in olive oil), or serve grilled or baked. They are excellent in soups and sauces and can replace cultivated mushrooms in any recipe.

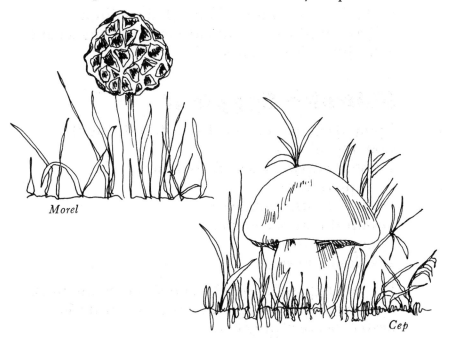

Morel

Cep

GRIOLLE, CHANTERELLE, CHANTRELLE or EGG MUSHROOM
(*Cantarellus cibarius*)

The griolle can be found dried or canned. It is wonderful just fried in butter with chopped onion, garlic, and parsley. It is also delicious in any of the recipes with eggs.

MATSUTAKE
(*Tricholoma matsutake*)

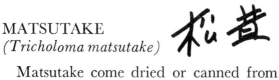

Matsutake come dried or canned from Japan, where they grow under pine trees (so they are called the *matsu,* or pine mushroom). Try in any of the shiitake recipes (see pp. 115, 116), or grilled.

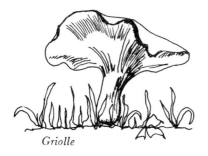

Griolle

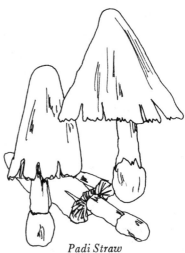

Padi Straw

PADI STRAW MUSHROOM
(Volvariella volvacea)

The padi straw mushroom comes dried from China, where it has been grown on beds of rice straw since ancient times. It is hard to find but sometimes it is obtainable in Chinese stores.

Soak 15 minutes in warm water. Substitute for shiitake (see pp. 115, 116).

TRUFFLE
(Tuber melanosporum)

Although they lose much of their flavor when canned, truffles are always a delicacy. They are best simmered in butter and eaten on their own.

WOOD EAR
(Auricularia polytricha)

You can buy wood ears dried, imported from China, where they are both collected and cultivated.

Soak for half an hour in tepid water. Rinse several times, separating the clusters to clean between them.

Use in any of the shiitake recipes (see pp. 115, 116).

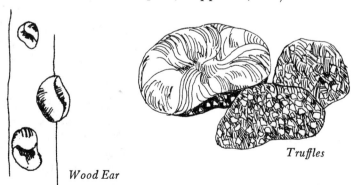

Truffles

Wood Ear

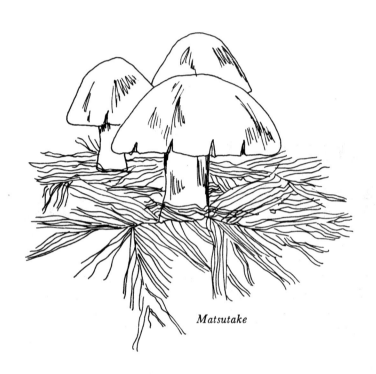

Matsutake

Chapter 16

Popular Wild Mushrooms

Since some mushrooms are poisonous, it is important to learn to recognize the edible varieties. It is advisable to use a reliable mushroom guide with color plates for this purpose.

The following is a list of the more common and popular of the wild mushrooms—should you be so fortunate as to find them.

HORSE MUSHROOM
(Agaricus arvensis)

The horse mushroom has a distinct anise odor, a sweetish taste and a tough flesh, which distinguishes it from the true meadow mushroom. Substitute in any of the recipes for cultivated mushrooms.

121

PARASOL MUSHROOM, UMBRELLA MUSHROOM
(Lepiota procera)

Parasol mushrooms are one of the finest of all edible mushrooms. Sometimes they can be found dried, imported from France. They are delicious fried or in a cream sauce. The English cook them open-side-down in a greased baking dish with sage and onion and butter, served with applesauce and roast potatoes. They are also good with fried eggs.

Horse   *Parasol*

FAIRY RING MUSHROOM, SCOTCH BONNET
(*Marasmius oreades*)

The fairy ring mushroom is found on lawns and grassy places, usually growing in circles or "fairy rings." It is especially good for mushroom soups and sauces.

PUFFBALL

The best puffballs are the very white barge puffballs, the engraved puffball or mosaic puffball, the grey-white, the pear-shaped, the pestle puffball, the warty and the pestle-shaped puffballs. They all should be eaten when fresh and young.

Serve them cut into slices dipped in egg and bread crumbs and fried in butter.

Puffball   *Fairy Ring*

SHAGGY CAP, SHAGGY MANE, INKY CAP
(Caprinus cornastres)

When the spores ripen the shaggy cap mushroom begins to liquefy. They should be eaten only when white and clean looking.

They are wonderful on a cream sauce served on toast. Or try them fried in butter and served on top of eggs in buttered ramekins, baked in the oven.

Shaggy Cap

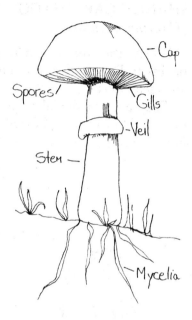

Glossary

As with any specialized field, there is a mushroom vocabulary consisting of scientific and technical terminology usually familiar only to professional botanists and growers. You may find it helpful to consult this list if you run into unfamiliar terms.

Activator: A bacteria which may be purchased to add to compost which speeds the composting process by greatly increasing the bacteria count in the compost.
Aerobic: With air; refering to bacteria which require air.
Agaricus bisporus: The domestic mushroom available in markets and to the home grower.
Anaerobic: Without air; referring to bacteria which thrive in air-free conditions.
Cap: (see mushroom diagram)

Casing: Covering the spawned compost with suitable materials to produce the mushroom fruiting.

Compost: Partly decomposed organic matter which supports the mushroom growth.

Flush: The appearance of mushrooms at intervals of about every two weeks.

Fruiting body: The mushrooms, including the cap and the stem.

Fumigation: Using chemical compounds to eradicate pests and diseases in the mushroom-growing house.

Fungus: Plants, including yeasts, molds, smuts and mushrooms, which gain nutrition usually from decaying organic matter.

Gills: (see mushroom diagram)

Hyphae: A fine thread-like growth which gives rise to the mycelium.

Lamella: Or gill (see mushroom diagram)

Mycelium: Threads which originate from the spawn and spread to permeate the compost and later fuse to form mushrooms.

Overcomposting: Preparing the compost past the point of maturation, resulting in a reduced crop.

Pasteurization or peak heating: Heating the compost and cropping area to between 130–140° for several hours. This absorbs excess moisture and drives pests to the surface to be killed by fumigation.

Spawn: Culture of mycelium used to start the growth of mushrooms in compost.

Spore: (see mushroom diagram)

Stem: (see mushroom diagram)

Synthetic composts: Composts made with various organic or inorganic compounds but without manure.

Undercomposting: Not allowing the composting process to reach its desired state of decomposition.

Veil: (see mushroom diagram)

List of Recipes